The Sleepover

Lynda J Pilon

The Sleepover
Copyright © 2021 by Lynda J Pilon

All rights reserved. No part of this publication may be reproduced, distributed, or transmitted in any form or by any means, including photocopying, recording, or other electronic or mechanical methods, without the prior written permission of the author, except in the case of brief quotations embodied in critical reviews and certain other non-commercial uses permitted by copyright law.

Tellwell Talent
www.tellwell.ca

ISBN
978-0-2288-5833-1 (Hardcover)
978-0-2288-4511-9 (Paperback)
978-0-2288-4512-6 (eBook)

For my granddaughter, Mackenna,
who was too young at the time to participate in this adventure.

Once upon a time, a long time ago, I think maybe it was just yesterday, three little children were excitedly packing their backpacks. They were going to their grandma and grandpa's farm for a sleepover.

"Now be good," said Claire and Andrew's mum.

Claire was four years old and her little brother Andrew was only two.

"We are going to be spoiled rotten," Claire happily informed her mother.

"AND WE WILL HAVE LOTS OF TREATS," bellowed Andrew. (He was very loud and only used his biggest outside voice.)

Down the street, their cousin Griffin was also impatiently waiting to be picked up. He was the same age as Claire. "We will stay up late and watch T.V.," Griffin told his mum.

"Do as Grandma and Grandpa say," warned his mother.

Soon the car arrived and off the three went with their grandma and grandpa.

The day went by very quickly. There was so much to do. Grandpa took them on a hayride. They played in the sandbox and rode their bikes. They made cupcakes with Grandma.

Bedtime came faster than Claire, Andrew, or Griffin wanted.

"We aren't tired," they said.

"Well, I'm tired," said Grandpa.

"I'm exhausted," said Grandma. "So, we are all going to bed."

"Will you sleep with us?" asked Griffin.

"We will be really good and not sneak out of bed," said Claire.

Andrew just jumped up and down on the bed.

"O.K.," said Grandma. "We will all sleep in the bunk bed room."

"That will be so much fun," giggled Claire. So, Claire, Andrew, and Griffin climbed into one bed, and Grandma and Grandpa climbed into the other.

"Tell us a story," they begged, and so Grandma told them the train story that they loved to hear.

"Goodnight, Claire. Goodnight, Andrew. Goodnight, Griffin. Love you guys," said Grandma.

"Goodnight, Grandma," they said. "Goodnight, Grandpa."

But Grandpa didn't say a word.

Instead, he let out loud pretend snores. Griffin, Claire, and Andrew shrieked with laughter, and immediately three more snoring sounds filled the room.

ZZZZZZZZZ   ZZZZZZZZZ   ZZZZZZZZZ

Grandma was not amused.

"Oh, for Pete's sake," said Grandma. "You will never get to sleep making this noise. It is time for all little snorers to go to sleep. Goodnight."

Grandma looked at Grandpa and gave him "the look." All was quiet.

THENNNNN

Grandpa started to toot. "Must have been the beans I had for supper," he said. Howls of laughter filled the air as sounds of toot, toot, TOOT, TOOOOOOOOOOOT were being made.

Andrew was jumping up and down on the bed. Claire was kicking her legs up in the air, and Griffin was sitting up in bed trying to make the loudest toot noise by blowing on his arm.

Grandma was not amused.

"Oh, for Pete's sake," said Grandma. "You will never get to sleep making this noise. It is time for all little tooters to stop."

Grandma looked at Grandpa and gave him "the look." All was quiet.

Grandma looked over at Grandpa who had instantly fallen fast asleep.

An hour later, the snoring, the tooting, the clawing, and the howling had gradually stopped. Everyone but Grandma was asleep.

"I think," sighed Grandma, "for the next sleepover, Grandpa will sleep in a room by himself."

www.ingramcontent.com/pod-product-compliance
Lightning Source LLC
LaVergne TN
LVHW071655060526
838200LV00029B/466